THESE ARE MY CHILDREN

These are my Children

Tony Cox

JEBELDALI

ISBN: 978-0-9511018-2-7

Published by: Jebeldali Press,
No.3, Bastwell House,
BLACKBURN,
Lancashire. BB1 9TE.

Printed in England by: Thomas Briggs (Blackburn) Ltd.,
37, King Street,
BLACKBURN,
Lancashire. BB2 2DH.

CONTENTS

For grown-ups

For children

Four cats

Love songs

People

For Grown-ups

These are my clocks.
They tell me the time
and tick out the metre
whilst I add the rhyme.

This is my garden
where every tree bears
both bittersweet almonds
and succulent pears.

These are my children.
They tell me the truth,
recalling the promises
made in my youth;

and this is my house,
wherein sleeps my love.
May to September
was not long enough.

New Year at Nancha

Nancha. Thousands, maybe millions,
of straight, strong pine trees
clothing the icy hillsides.
Through them, the steep, winding track of steel.

It snowed gently for several minutes
after each train had laboured by
as clouds of steam drifted across
the frosted landscape.
Trainloads of huge logs and other,
hidden merchandise,
going from somewhere
to we-knew-not-where.

Citizens, comrades, well wrapped in fur,
going about their daily lives,
seemingly heedless of the bitter cold.

Locomotives plaintively calling
to each other in the yard,
all day, all night, like whales;
the mournful songs of powerful, yet gentle,
doomèd creatures.

In the cold, candle-lit evening,
Oona, newly appointed to the new hotel,
cooked and served our meal
then shyly sang for us,
a sorrowful, sweet, melodious song
and let us take her photograph.

On reading
"The dance that suffers from hard work"
by Saw Wai

These words might never fall
upon the ears of the people.
They make their slow
unsteady progress
mostly in the dark of silence.

These dreams might never pass
before the eyes of the people,
may not even dance briefly
on the flickering screen of Time
between advertisements
for junk-food and motor-cars.

Will they be heard or seen again
before their language changes,
with a different script
and different meanings,
or even before the worms of Time
chew up the rough pages
on which they live today?

Will a single image,
captured by chance
in his beloved, hidden town
that cries for rice and water,
convey one shaft of meaning
to some other mind or brain
pausing, then passing, in the train
to Mandalay?

Nightmare

I jumped in the dark
from the top of Horsehold Rocks
without a parachute;
counted only two, tugging the imaginary rip-cord.
"Come on, men. Don't be afraid.
Hang on to your rifles. Follow me!"

An age in the sickening blackness
of the night;
the jagged ground waiting below
to convert my dream
into the terrifying blindness
of eternity.

I waken to the half-light
of our bedroom before dawn;
moan of wind in the chimney
and the reassuring warmth
of you beside me,
sleeping.

Punctuation

I ask myself, *"Is Death*
a full stop or a comma?"
Getting no dependable reply
but only dread of one
and hope of t'other,
go to ask the priest, old Simon's mother,
Doctor Phillips and the man next door.

None of them is very sure.
Indeed, they seem to wonder what I'm selling.

Is the punctuation, though,
what really matters?
(Surely not the spelling?)
Maybe the preceding sentence,
life, is more important;
possibly its content, purpose, context . . . .

Get the syntax right
and let the punctuation
take care of itself.

Anyway, suppose I *were* to press
in error the wrong key
on this dilapidated typewriter
which tells my life,
then would I be eradicated instantly?
Or is the use of backspace
and correction fluid still
a possibility?

Taxila Junction

I sat at the top of the hill
above Taxila Junction
and watched the noon train
leave for Havelian.

I watched for seven miles
until the smoke was just a smudge
in the shimmering haze
on the horizon near Haripur.

All that time,
goats were risking their lives
to eat thorns
from the tough and wiry bushes
on the hot rocks
and precipitous slopes;
one small boy,
playing on a simple flute,
to guard them.

The sun was merciless
and I some kind of fool
to have only a copy
of last week's *Manchester Guardian*
to shield me from its heat.

I should have stayed below,
in the shade
by the pool of huge goldfish in the temple of Wah
but I was hungry for the wider view.

Do not talk to me of quarks.

We can no more comprehend
the countless discrete influences
which constitute a charm
than know the past details
or future course of the lives
of the twenty persons perched
atop the second carriage
of the Havelian train.

Do not tell me about black holes.

There have been so many thoughts
written or spoken
on this inhabited speck so far today
that it is already no longer possible
for the brightest spirit
to escape their gravity.

Anyway,
who believes in quarks and black holes
but the most deluded alchemist,
or possibly the children perched aloft
upon the noon train to Havelian?

Tain l'Hermitage
(forty years on . . . .)

I sat near the hilltop
above the hermitage of Tain
and watched the noon train
leave for Avignon.

No-one on the carriage roofs this time.
Few inside, I guessed,
though I was much too far away to see.
I watched for only three miles
until I saw the swift snake swallowed
by the trees bordering the motorway.

All that time,
fat barges were drifting down the Rhône
as distant hum of traffic
wafted up the hill to where I sat
whilst brown and orange butterflies
flittered, somewhat aimlessly, I thought,
from nowhere in particular to nowhere
and slender lizards darted
from shade to shadow.

The sun was merciless,
ripening the grapes
of *Monsieur Chapoutier*
and I some kind of fool
to have chosen
that time of day
to explore his hill.

Do not tell me there was a Big Bang
from which all came.

Far more likely
some Celestial Craftsman
fashioned this universe
on forges far beyond our comprehension.

Do not tease me with talk
of unimaginable calamities
engendered by the wings of butterflies.

Before such perturbation of the air
could travel half a mile
the weight of countless
words and thoughts
would surely dampen
and eliminate its ardour.

Anyway,
who believes in Big Bangs
and butterfly-begotten cataclysms
but the most deluded alchemist?

There is plenty else
for us to care about.
Will the noon train get to Avignon on time
and was, indeed, its transit of this valley curve
only for these eyes to see?

Spectrum

Colours we call red
are blood and poppies;
cherries, rubies and, it could be said,
fury, fire or breast of robins.

Colours we call blue
are sea and sky;
indigo and cobalt, harebells too;
misery and lapis lazuli.

Colours we call yellow;
butter, lemon,
turmeric, canary, primrose;
cowardice and brimstone.

All these three make black;
ebony and jet, raven, crow.
Deep despair at Winter's dark.

Or all of them make white;
chalk, milk, ivory and snow.
Purity and hope and light.

Summer day

In this hot sunshine,
Blackburn is Rome.
Light-bulbs are water-fruit;
anywhere is home.

In this bright sunlight,
Salford is Venice.
Barges are elephants;
shadows play tennis.

In the tall forest,
back of beyond,
warm breezes, butterflies,
chapel bells' sound.

Dreams are for everyone
in this fair land.
Door-knobs are ladybirds;
strike up the band.

     *   *   *   *

In this bright moonlight,
Manchester blooms.
Leopards lie drowsy
in hot, shady rooms.

Children asleep now,
today's work is done.
Dreams are their catapults,
anywhere is home
and the seven hills of Blackburn
look up to the moon.

Stone's lament

I am alone.
I am a stone
sitting on a planet of sand and stones.

But this is no place to be a stone.
I'm not appreciated
and there's no living here for stones.

I want to go to Hebden Bridge,
West Yorkshire, England, Earth,
where they build their homes,
roads, chimneys and chapels
of stones like me
and stones are appreciated for what they are
and what they can be.

I've heard of stones in England, Earth,
fashioned into birds, dead admirals and saints,
some with fine words inscribed upon them.
Oh! What a life for a stone!
I would be happy, very happy, there
even as a humble kerb or step or lintel.

Perhaps I could aspire to be a rounded stone
over which splashes the cool water
of a stream laced with foam and fishes;
or even a stepping stone upon which children
cross unsteadily, squealing with delight,
my shoulder slicing the waters confidently.

Or what about a wishing stone,
showered with bright coins
and fondled by young lovers
hoping I will give them
what they think they want?

It would be enough for me
just sitting at a mountain top
to silently survey the lovely Earth
in company with other happy stones;
maybe someday racing helter-skelter
down the steep slopes
to terrify the goats
and make the hawks and eagles
jump into the sky
shrieking and squawking.

I could even mark and guard
the final resting place
of someone who was loved
or did some good . . . .
So many possibilities in England, Earth.

Here, I'm just a worthless, lonely stone,
doomed to stay, perhaps forever,
on this cold planet of sand and stones.

May, July, October, Death

SPRING

This is my season of glory.
Yes, now I feel the sunshine warm
upon these frost-weary boughs, mine arms,
and May is come.
Winter's never-ending night is done.

These already-swollen buds
crowded, itching, on my fingertips
since Autumn
(all of the Winter aching, aching)
suddenly next week will properly awaken
and burst out in blossom,
pink and white.

Winter's never-ending night is gone.
Vagrant birds are nestling,
singing, scuffling here within
mine armpits and the interstices of my twigs,
their intricately-fashioned homes
precariously founded in the temperate glades
and cloisters of my new-grown leaves.

Yes, now I feel the sunshine hot upon my soul.
This whole season I'll give shade and shelter
to all kind of lost and hungry creature,
for this is the time of plenty.
May is come.

*   *   *   *

SUMMER

July follows June.
Brief orange-hazy heat of Summer.
This is the joy, the pinnacle, the peak,
the ecstasy and exultation;
Hallelujah Chorus.

This is our true glory, our July.
Improvident, unthinking multitudes
Will bask in its hot passion
not suspecting just how shallow
is the cup of their fulfilment.

It's not for me,
(I've lived and loved five hundred such Julys),
to tell these creatures now
how brief their taste of happiness
must be.

It's not for me,
(I've died five hundred such Julys),
to warn them of the future.

*   *   *   *

AUTUMN

Autumn closes now upon their lives and mine.
Swallows and swifts have flown;
long since packed their memories
of Summer's glories –
gone to warmer climes.
Squirrels hasten to gather and store
their final fruits and rinds.
No longer can I hold my leaves
against the brutal strength
and bluster of the new-born wind.

This year's fast-maturèd young
who never knew a Winter,
feel through their mother's ribs
a strange, wild quickening of the heart
and wonder what it's all about.

Yellow frogs have come
to snuggle in the crevices
between my toes,
beneath my fallen leaves,
in moss as warm as slippers.

A fast-declining sun
strikes horizontally across the shaven fields,
hardly to warm the bark upon
my black, uplifted branches.

O what can I give now
to the less fortunate,
the careless creatures of this world,
rootless and oppressed?

Only that I'm here, always here,
always present for the show next year;
a living, branchèd rock, arms already laden
with tiny embryonic miracles, aching promises
of new life to come next May,
buds of Heaven sleeping on my twigs . . . .

*   *   *   *

DEATH

. . . . until, suddenly,
one day or night,
I shall be split asunder by some lightning bolt,
my time of reckoning come
and I shall be from then merely a sentinel,
invaded by Death's fungus;
beetles scuttling through the empty sockets
of my limbs and eyes.

Merely a stark sentinel I shall remain a while,
at best a dark, occasional reminder
to the world's complacent occupants
of what's to be;
or, more likely, just a post
on which the conceited stag
may sharpen and test his antlers.

Amen.

Busy, busy

I'm drawing up a list of *"Things to do"*
for ticking off as things are done.
Commence, at number one,
with *"Start a list of things to do"*.

Best thing to write as item two –
well, why not *"Tick off, when completed, number one"*?
These can be cleared quite quickly then.
Two things done;
the day hardly begun.

I'll rest now, let the cat out,
have a cup of tea, update my list.

For item number three, now let me see –
perhaps it should be *"Take a break"*?
"Let the cat out" can be four.
"Have a drink of tea" at number five
with *"Contemplate my list"* at six.

Every item detailed
makes me realize how much I've done
and how much more there's still to do.
Better stop again, for coffee now
and let the cat back in.

Shall I put those on the list?
No. Don't be silly.
That would be absurd.
That would be
bureaucracy gone mad.

Sunday dream

Old men sleeping in the afternoon.
Her eyes pierce the back of my head.
"Your neck is bent.
Two points better than a straight one.
Look at me."
I race for the next alley.
Bricks lying on the ground.
Were they put there? Did they fall?

Camera crew running backwards
recording my thoughts;
recording the sleeping bricks
and old men pretending to sleep.
Were those bricks put there,
one on top of the other?
Are they feigning sleep?

We come to the bell tower,
stand below the bell,
chanting in a language
that we do not understand.
Adorning the walls are portraits
of the women I have loved.
The bell tolls.
We go inside, repeat it all.
Did she follow me?

The old men are getting up now
to join us in the hall,
abandoning the dreaming bricks.
The bell stops ringing. The recitation stops.
I am awake. Seven o'clock.
How did it start?
Where is the girl who loves me?

For Children

Visitor

Whence comes the wind now
and why pass this way?
What does it want here?
How long will it stay?

Why does this wind blow
and with so much force;
bending the willow
and shaking the gorse?

By whom was this wind sent
and what does it find;
rattling the casement
and rippling the blind?

What can the wind do
in boisterous play,
racing to get to
tomorrow today?.

*   *   *

Where did the wind go
and why in such haste;
whirling the leaves so
then slamming the gate?

We hoped it would show
us its masterful plan.
What does the wind know
that we never can?

The pit

Well, then I dug this hole, you see
and everyone fell in but me.
I filled it up with earth and stones
to make quite sure I'd be alone

and all the world belonged to me;
all the fields and every tree.
I sang and skipped and felt divine.
The whole wide universe was mine.

But after only half a day
I needed somebody to play
at hide-and-seek with, so I tried
to find the hole with everyone inside.

I searched the hills and forest floor.
I've looked for it along the shore.
It's just no use at all because
I can't remember where it was.

Unhappy me! Betrayed, forlorn!
Forever I shall be alone!
No-one loves me, no-one cares
how bored I am, how I despair.

O desert world, no friends, no fun.
O devil spade, O selfish everyone
to leave me in this lonely hell.
Dear Hole, come swallow me as well.

Inside the piano

Inside the piano a strange smell.
What it is I cannot tell
but this I know and know full well;

it's not quite rats, nor bats, nor cats;
not fleas, nor bumblebees, nor cheese.

It's not dry rot, nor apricot,
nor something that the dog forgot.

It could be wood or Christmas pudd.
More likely just some dust or rust.

Anyway, no more delay!
This instrument is here to stay.
What it smells of, who can say?
Just close the top and let us play.

Alien intruders

One day last week
I saw the field behind our house
invaded by a gang
of great big noisy yellow things.

They quickly made themselves at home,
dug out some comfortable holes and then
began to play a complicated game
with bricks and blocks and lengths of string.

One scraped and scooped the muddy ground,
another carted slates and planks around.
A late arrival, churning as it came
a concrete pudding, tipped it on the floor
then went straight off to get some more.

They all made fearful, growling, grumbling sounds
except the crane, which swivelled stiffly to and fro
amongst them, helping here and there –
impatient yellow monsters bustling down below,
bumping, clanking, snorting everywhere.

All in all, it was a very busy scene –
but I preferred the back field green.

In the Land of Bong

"Birds fly backwards in the Land of Bong."
"Upside down and sideways too where I come from."

"We have oak trees two miles high."
"We have weeds which scrape the sky."

"Buttercups are blue in the Land of Bong."
"So are the moon and stars where I come from."

"I earn twenty pounds a year."
"I get forty and a coach and pair."

"Everyone drinks wine in the Land of Bong."
"We drink whiskey, gin and rum
and fight and quarrel all night long."

"We don't do that in the Land of Bong."

Ditty

Dan, Dan,
(a whimsical man),
did steal a pig
and away he ran
to Heckmondwig.

Dan, Dan,
from the prison van
did shout an oath
at Butcher Ben
and Big-eye Len,
(both whimsical men),
of Heckmondwig.

Relations

When relations visit us
they never use the door.
They slide in down the chimney
or come up through the floor.

We make them feel unwelcome
by feeding poisoned fish.
They eat it up and ask for more
then gobble up the dish.

Mister Slug

Underneath my rhubarb,
I met a giant slug.
I smiled at him, wished him *"Good day"*,
gave him a little hug.

But he was in a surly mood
and wrinkled up his skin.
He didn't answer, not one word
and pulled his horns right in.

"Well, if you feel like that," I said,
"I've other things to do."
I felt a little bit upset
so poked him with my shoe.

At this, he flew into a rage.
*"For that act you must pay.
I'll eat your rhubarb, leaves and all."*
(Well, what else could he say?)

"Whilst you are fast asleep," he said,
*"I'll eat your cabbage too.
The day you mess with Mister Slug
is one day you will rue."*

Jim, jam, jollywog

Jim, jam, jollywog,
catch a bird, chase a hog.
Watch the salmon leaping.
Don't waste time a-sleeping.

Jim, jam, jollywog,
stroke a cat, race a dog.
Don't let life go creeping by.
Don't waste time a-sleeping.

Jim, jam, jollywog,
hunt the wind, split a log.
Hours and minutes are for reaping.
Don't waste them a-sleeping.

Jim, jam, jollywog,
bang a drum, drain a bog.
No need now for weeping.
Don't waste time a-sleeping.

Jim, jam, jollywog,
tame a sparrow, paint a frog.
Time's for spending, not for keeping.
Don't waste it a-sleeping.

Don't waste time a-sleeping.

I wish we had a cow

I wish we had a cow.
She would not say *"Wuff-wuff, bow-wow"*.
She'd lie upon the hearth-rug
as quiet as can be
and chew her last week's breakfast
until tomorrow's tea.

I wish we had a cow.
She would not *"tweet"* nor say *"Miaow"*.
She wouldn't mess the cushions
nor scratch the piano top.
She'd lick the stamps for letters
and fetch things from the shop.

Mine eyes fell out

Mine eyes fell out onto the floor.
They ran across the carpet
and under the door.
They never came back
to tell me what they saw.

Four Cats

Next-door's cat

O lovely big pussy-cat,
sitting in the tree,
why don't you come down
to play with me?
I'll help you catch
a mouse for tea
and chase the silly
dogs away
if you agree.

The pussy-cat, he smiled
as though to say
he'd like to come
right down to play
but just for now
he'd rather stay
up in his tree.
So let it be
another day.

Transmogrification

Oh no! My pussy-cat is upside down.
Her furry feet wave in the air.
How can I take her into town?
Wow! That *would* make the people stare.

Her little legs wave in the air,
her tiny claws clutch at the sky.
My pussy-cat fell off her chair.
I hope and pray she will not die.

      *   *   *   *

What now? I can't believe mine eyes.
My pussy-cat is inside out –
she's smooth and only half the size.
I'll have to buy her a new coat.

Her tiny head turned inside out,
her tongue and ears will meet;
her whiskers tickerling her throat.
It must be difficult to eat.

      *   *   *   *

At last! My pussy-cat is on her feet
and furry once again.
Now I can walk her down the street
or take her on the train.

My latest cat

Now my latest cat
is as blind as a bat
and he hangs upside down on a nail in the wall.

Oh, he catches the mice
and eats peaches and rice
but he's no good at fishing at all, at all,
(well, he's not bad for someone so small).

He seems to take flight
when he's put out at night
and I'm worried in case he should trip up and fall.

He dives through the trees
with the greatest of ease
but I've not heard him purring at all, at all,
(such a cat I don't ever recall).

I bought him a lead,
rubber bone and some seed
and I've taught him to fetch back a stick or a ball,

but I think he's a freak
and since Tuesday last week
I just haven't seen him at all, at all,
(and he still doesn't come when I call).

Night cat

I love my pussy-cat so very much
and wanted her to know how much I care.
I wondered, should I liberate her
from the endless tedium of sleeping by the fire?

Should I stop her being lazy
and encourage her to jump and shout;
let her drive the cat-flap crazy,
dodging in and out?

What about a trip to Blackpool,
climb the tower, see the sea;
eat some rock and fluffy sugar,
maybe fish and chips for tea?

But how well do I know my cat
and what she's *really* like?
I got up late last night to find out what she's at
whilst I'm in bed asleep.

Was she playing with a catapult
or pawing through a catalogue? Does she sing
a catchy tune while strutting down the cat-walk
as she gazes at a king?

I found her drinking mousy milk
before the television, softly sighing when
yet more catastrophes were heaped
on Tom by Jerry once again.

I hadn't realized before, that
if I'd let *her* choose,
she'd always watch the weather-for-cats
following the late night mews.

Love Songs

Days when I see Jean

Sunshine fills the attics of my mind
the days when I see Jean.
It rains the hollow times between.

Should I stand quite still
and watch as water gathers on the window-sill
or spend such dreary days
in cultivating fantastic gardens
in plant-pots and jam-jars?

Comets light the corners of my dreams
the nights when I see Jean.
No stars the dismal times between.

Should I lie alone 'til noon,
not sleeping, wishing idly for a silver moon
or spend such melancholy days
in polishing the brass knobs
and steel railing of my bed?

Through the open skylight
of my mind today, at dawn,
I heard the music, saw the lawns of heaven
filled with singing-birds.
All is vibrant, yet serene.
Today I'll see my Jean.

Walking in the rain

Underneath my umberella,
me and Jean, out in the rain,
all alone and close together,
walking, dreaming, up the lane.

Shelter of this umberella
keeps our hopes and secrets dry,
when we go out dreaming, walking
in the rain, my Jean and I.

No-one knows where we are going,
no-one guesses where we've been,
lost beneath my umberella,
Jean and I, just me and Jean.

In love

In love we lie together
and the music on the radio
has faded low then swelled again
to fill my soul with feelings
that I cannot put a name to,
only 'love'.

The singer's words, not filtered by my mind,
have flown directly to my heart
with meanings that I cannot comprehend.
I turn my head and there you are,
asleep upon my pillow,
deep in love.

I see your long hair tumbled on my arm.
If you wake, I know you'll smile to see me here;
I know you'll snuggle closer, dear,
and fall asleep again.
Home is where you are
and warm is love.

Marianne

One day I always shall remember
(I think that day my life began),
the sunny morning last September
when I first met you, Marianne.

Since then you've figured all my dreams
and wishes, stimulated every plan.
Although I never see you now, it seems
I never can forget you, Marianne.

Animal magnetism

I walk towards you and the music
in my lodestone heart grows stronger.
When I leave you, so the magic
fades, regaling me no longer.

I'd say my heart's a mine-detector;
that would faithfully define
the feeling but not quite the fact –
unfortunately, you're not mine!

What shall I be?

Oh, shall I be wild for you tonight, my love?
Shall I wear my tiger jacket, bright pink socks;
conceal a dozen wicked jackdaws
in my sleeves and pockets
ready to fly out shrieking at some given signal?
Shall I play hilarious jokes on all our friends,
walk upside down upon my hands,
scattering the dishes on the tabletop,
astounding all the waiters?
Shall I be wild for you tonight?

Or shall I play it cool tonight, my love,
remote; apparently indifferent
to all the world outside;
calm and quiet in the cloisters of our unity?
Two white-breasted doves
shall be our gentle and restrainèd conversation.
Drifting waiters hardly dare approach
lest they might breach
the closeness of our love.
Shall I be cool for you tonight?

Or shall I be myself tonight,
for this auspicious evening
when we two in love shall dine together,
fingers solemnly entwined?
Shall I balance carefully between
these other selves, the wild, the cool,
just me exposed and loving you,
loving you beyond all need
for masks or show?
Shall I be myself tonight, my love?

This locked and rusty box

This locked and rusty box, my heart,
is full of dreams and hopes. The key cannot belong
to anyone, I thought, not even you or me –
I the Singer, you the Song.

Last night, I wished that we might find
the special rhyme or counterpoint which we should sing
to charm it open, some incongruous duet –
I the Autumn, you the Spring.

Before you left, you somehow touched
the secret switch and accidentally released
the long-forgotten fairy-tale I kept inside –
you the Beauty, I the Beast.

All you want

I'd like to show you my collection
    of rare cycads
and the medals and awards received
    for dancing over swords,
but all you want is love.

I mean to give you frankincense
    and gold and myrrh,
and teach you how to make a tiger purr
    by ruffling up its fur,
but what you crave is love.

I'll give you amulets and silken scarves
    and rings and beads;
show you how they built the pyramids
    and where to find the Pleiades,
but what you need is love.

I whisper tales of travel
    to exotic lands;
take you to Troy and Samarkand;
    play music for you
    as a one-man-band,
but all you listen for is love.

      *   *   *   *

Darkness comes and sweet perfume
    invades the room.
Parting clouds reveal the moon.
    It's not too soon
to give you all my love.

People

Freida

There was this girl in the Spanish class.
She was from the Philippines, I think,
and very pretty,
with spectacles only half hiding
her lovely eyes.

We had to choose Spanish names for ourselves
which weren't our own.
I can't remember why.

Anyway, she called herself Freida
(after Freida Kahlo, she said).
I don't know whether she had been to Mexico
or just liked the pictures in a Freida Kahlo book
borrowed from the library.
Why did I never ask?

I always chose her, if I could,
to be my partner in the tests.
She was much better than me
at remembering what day it was (in Spanish),
the names of the months
and how to give directions
to the railway station.

But then I was ill and missed five weeks.
I did go back once
but had no hope of catching up
and anyway she wasn't there.

My head has not been turned

My head has not been turned now I am rich.
I'm quite determined to remain unspoiled,
completely unaffected by the untold wealth
which so fortuitously came my way.

I *have* obtained a somewhat larger,
though still modest, house, of course,
but this is necessary so that I can give
a full expression to my innate generosity –
parties for my new-found friends
and adequate accommodation
for the homely treasures
which have gathered late about me.

I *do* still relish all the simple pleasures
of the senses – wholesome smell
of new-mown carpet in the hall,
the splishing, splashing music
of the dry martini waterfall
and sunlight sparkling from the gold-encrusted
decorations on the wall.

I've *still* no special servant
just employed to say *"Good morning"*
and *"Good-night, sleep well, God bless"*
to all my pets and children.
I can use my own voice for this task,
conserving it, of course,

as far as possible by utilizing (when appropriate)
solicitors to dot and double-dot mine "i"s
and cross my tees before I come to them;
accountants who may lisp in deferential tones
the joyous totals of mine interest and income
whilst the minstrel choir reverberates the walls
recalling hymns of praise received
in statements sent by Lloyds and Barclays.

Each and every morning I still wind,
myself, my clockwork nightingales.
When topping up their reservoirs of liquid song,
I say to each and every one of them:
"Whom do you love, O Philomel Clockworkius?
Is it me you love above all others?"
"Yes", they sing. *"Yes, yes"* their sweet replies.

And here, electric dogs with ever-greeting eyes
and faithful tails which wag
when only my step nears
(their bellies full of sovereigns).
"Down, Solenoid", and *"Down!"*, I say
with firm and unmistakable authority of tone
which comes quite naturally from a man
of substance and simplicity like me.

Oh yes. I'm quite determined
to remain unspoiled now I am rich.
My head has not been turned.

Thornley, G.

Thornley, G.,
O Thornley, G.,
(of lovely leg
and gorgeous knee),
will you come out to play with me
and maybe come back home for tea?

You'll get to know my cat and see
what I am really like and what can be.

I hope you'll come
to live with me
so I can pamper and adore
your lovely hip and thigh and knee
forevermore.

Thornley, G.,
O Thornley, G..

Albert William Jeremy Hall

Albert William Jeremy Hall
loved Lisa dearly; thought he always would;
wrote "Jeremy loves Lisa" on the wall.
He wrote it large and wide and proud.

Unfortunately, when it rained,
the love for Lisa washed out of his heart
and long before the moon had waned
his loins were drawn to Judy Smart.

A pity then he wrote in paint
of love now demonstrably chalk.
The words upon the wall cannot grow faint
so dogs will mew and cats must bark.

Treasures

Look! A pair of scissors which will not cut!
I've had them for many years.
They were very cheap
but now have great sentimental value.

And here,
my collection of pebbles.
I love their textures and colours.
Some are very smooth
and see – this one – you turn it in the light,
it glistens with streaks like gold.
These stones are worth nothing
but I wouldn't be without them.

And look at these dried leaves
which I've collected myself
and pressed between the pages of a book.
I know their names.
When I have time,
they will be pasted to a board
to make a sort of picture.

Piled in the garden I have old rubber tyres.
Some still have fancy treads, all different.
They could be used in many ways
and they cost me nothing.
Mister Greenwood gave them to me
when he moved to Bacup.

There, behind the shed, are stacked
ceramic sinks and sturdy buckets,
(galvanised; they will not rust)
and corrugated aluminium tubs.
They will definitely come in useful.

I also have small bars of soap
obtained by my aunt
from hotels in foreign lands,
(they were all free),
and pens which no longer write
but which have names and badges
on the sides.

Willow pattern plates
of different sizes;
not cracked nor stained.
I know the story.

Old bus tickets of the
Todmorden Joint Omnibus Committee;
just look at all these colours –
orange, green, black-and-red, blue-and-brown.

They are all treasures to me.

I'm short of nothing.

Where have you been?
(freely translated from the Yorkshire dialect)

Oh yes. I went to Ilkley
just to see the famous moor,
to walk thereon without my hat.
I'm young and healthy;
what was there to fear?

Anyway, I hadn't even reached
the first ridge of the hill
when suddenly this frightful Yorkshire gale
arose, reached down and plucked
right off my back my coat,
my woolly scarf
and shirt and socks as well.

The robust Yorkshire germs
of influenza, hypothermia and worse
attacked at once
and long before I'd time to think
of Freddy Truman, I was gone.

Naked, I descended gloomily to Hell.
This wasn't my intention after all.

Hardly was I buried when
the fearsome Yorkshire worms
came wiggling, waggling in
and ate mc up.

Predictably, of course, a flock
of ravenous Yorkshire ducks
came quacking, swooping quickly down
to gobble up these worms.

Then who should happen by
but Sutcliffe, with his trusty shotgun.
Only once he fired and every duck
did plummet to the Yorkshire ground.

So ponder this as you pour out the Beaujolais
and genteel conversation ebbs and flows
across the polished table-top;
the duck sublime you eat
as prelude to the Yorkshire Pudd. and stuffing
and upon whose subtle taste and texture
you will compliment the chef,
has within it
richly interwoven molecules of me,
your late departed friend.

Was this a worthwhile end?

Mr. Prickletwist

I like that Mister Prickletwist.
His hair is thick and greasy.
He doesn't bother much with girls
(unless he's sure they're easy).

I like that Mister Prickletwist.
I think he likes my sister.
He also likes Joanna Jones;
(well, anyway, he kissed her).

I like that Mister Prickletwist.
His arms are fat and hairy.
They reach down low, beyond his knees.
(He needs them long for Mary).

I like that Mister Prickletwist,
although his face is gruesome;
(but so is mine, or so they say.
We'd make an ideal twosome).

I *love* that Mister Prickletwist.
I know he'd bring me sorrow,
but if he were to ask me to,
I'd marry him tomorrow.

Mrs. Notnice

Next-door-but-one lived Missis Notnice,
(slugs and snails, not sugar nor spice).
She didn't like children, nor rabbits, nor cats
and ate lots of thistles, lice, toads and bats.

She made me sprout both spots and warts,
caused me to have unwholesome thoughts;
turned eternal truth to lies,
teed my dots and crossed her thighs.

Next-door-but-one Missis Notnice lived.
She loved all things horrid, on hatred she thrived.
She pickled skylarks in their nests.
Accountants and lawyers were her guests.

She never tried, complained "I can't".
She said "things are" which plainly aren't.
She spun huge webs, ate cockroach pies
and tossed her dots to tease mine eyes.

Next-door-but-one lived Missis Notnice.
She hated small kittens, robins and mice.
Scorpion sandwiches, hedgehogs on toast,
these are what she loved the most.

Mrs. Googlebot

I fell for Missis Googlebot
(lots of buttocks,
   mighty thighs and knees);
when we kissed, the redolence
of Gorgonzola cheese.

She had a crooked nose and hammer-toes,
small, piggy eyes
   and yellow teeth;
hefty hips to google with
and much, much more beneath.

I sighed all day and dreamed of her all night.
I dreamed of romping
   in a giant cot,
(hot music on the radio),
just me with Missis Googlebot.

Throughout that Spring, each day, all day,
I longed for Missis Googlebot.
   Alas, it could not be;
for she could google, I could not
and she's forsaken me.

Peter Parsley

Peter Parsley lived in Barnsley
all his life.
He took Meg Marrowfat of Stairfoot
for his wife.

Saw the trains leave Court House station
every day;
often wondered where they went to,
far away.

Watched the racing pigeons loaded
in the van;
knew they flew back home to Barnsley,
every one.

When the rain fell on the cobbles
all day long,
he always thought it sang a very
cheerful song.

Sowed nasturtiums in his garden,
lupins too;
saw them daily splashed from heaven.
How they grew!

Peter Parsley lived in Barnsley
all his life.
He loved the trains, the rain, his garden
and his wife.

Peter Parsley died in Barnsley.

It's alright for you

Look at me.
I'm sitting on the top of a pole,
uncomfortable, precarious,
my meals brought to me on a long stick.

It's alright for you.
You can go home whenever you like;
sit by the fire or weed the garden;
eat your dinner, play golf
or stroke the cat
and go to bed to sleep at night.

Me. I have to perch,
precariously, uncomfortably,
on top of this pole
for as long as it takes,
cold in the dreary darkness,
roasted by the sun in the daytime.
And what about . . . . ?
Don't ask! It's not a hollow pole.

It's alright for you,
cosy in your armchair by the television,
watching the news about people
sitting on the tops of poles,
uncomfortable, precarious,
justifying their existence as individuals.
It's alright for you.

*   *   *   *

Look at me.
I'm hitting my head with a big hammer.
Yes, it hurts, of course,
but it's alright for you.

*   *   *   *

Look at me.
I'm swimming naked in a tank
with starving sharks . . . .

Grandad's lullaby

Ready for bed now,
guests are all gone.
Moon's in the attic,
today's work is done.

Teeth in the bucket
under the stair;
wig on the bed-rail,
socks on the chair.

Reach down the bottle
of dreams from the shelf.
Sink deep in the pillow,
all by yourself.

Coda

Fishes, fruit, bread and wine;
catchy tunes, careless talk.
Dogs are yours, cats are mine;
loops and oblongs, cheese and chalk.

Take the train to Happyday,
Cherry Tree and Pleasington.
Come back round the other way,
by Rose Grove and Simonstone.

Stars and lakes; hopes, wishes;
towers, flowers, trees and birds.
Wind the clock and wash the dishes;
hasty actions, fickle words.

Change at Preston, change at Crewe;
haunting music, rivers flow.
Do what only you can do
but go where all the others go.

Honeysuckle, pears and pine.
Brian, Brian, Ronnie, Seth.
I am yours and she is mine;
stone, paper, scissors, death.

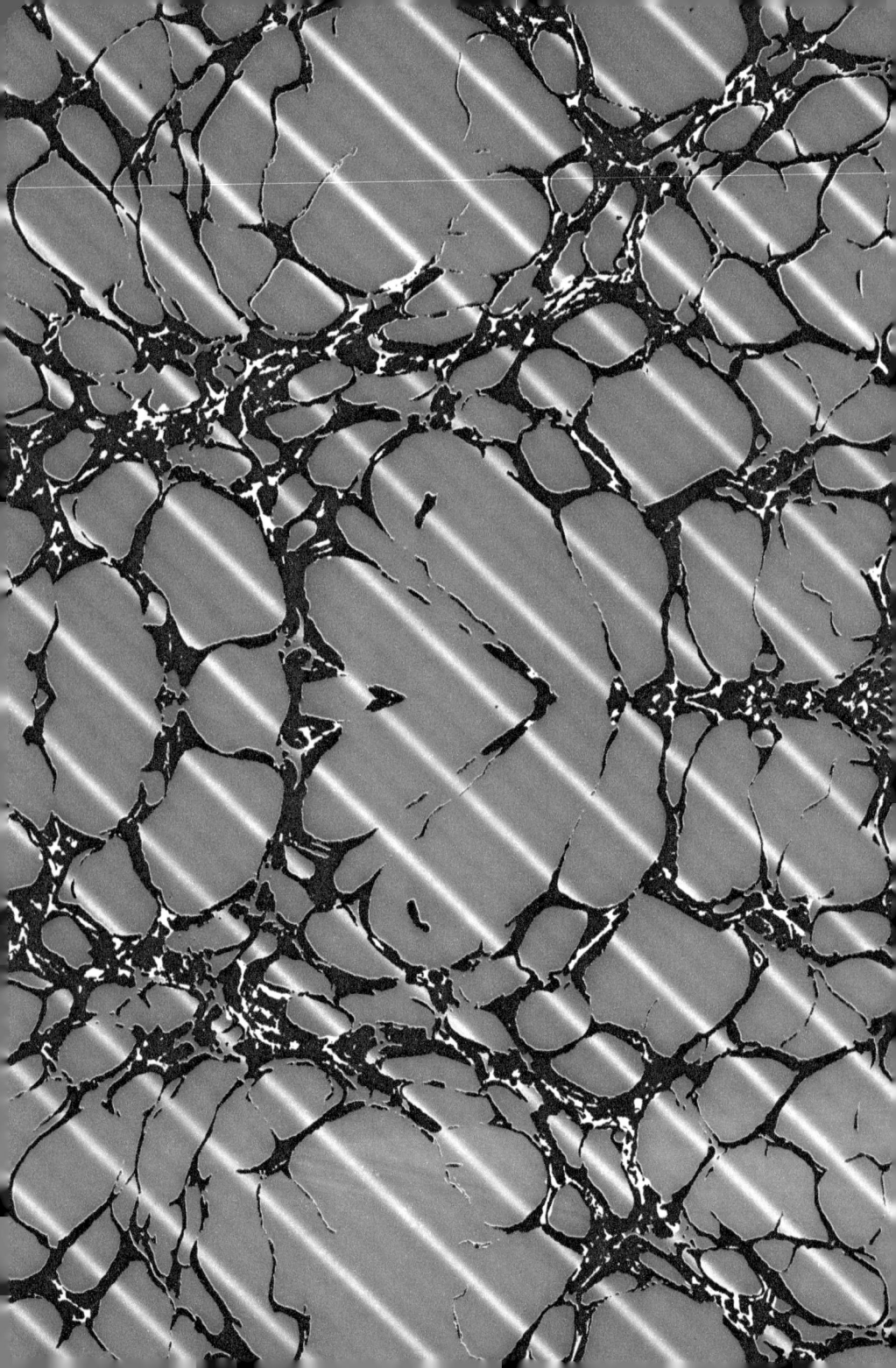